MW00396164

Dedicated to all the students, parents, guardians and educators
that have influenced me to teach with transparency, authority
and most of all from the heart.
It's not all about what you teach or how you teach
but it's also about the way you inspire others to
pursue their dreams along the way.

Key Terms

Entrepreneur - a person who organizes and manages any enterprise, especially a business, usually with considerable initiative and risk.

Influencer - a person who has the power to influence many people, as through social media

Niche - a place or position suitable or appropriate for a person or thing. A distinct segment of a market.

Brainstorm - a sudden impulse, idea

Strategic - important in or essential to strategy

Process - a systematic series of actions directed to some end

Service - an act of helpful activity; help; aid

Product - a thing produced by labor

Consumer/consumer avatar - a person or organization that uses a commodity or service; ideal customer

Target audience - the persons reached by a business, book, radio or television broadcast, etc

Key Terms

Market - an open place or a covered building where buyers and sellers convene for the sale of goods

Brand - kind, grade, or make, as indicated by a stamp, trademark, or the like

Logo - a graphic representation or symbol of a company name, trademark, abbreviation,etc., often uniquely designed for ready recognition.

Employed - to hire or engage the services of (a person or persons)

Unemployed - without a job; out of work

Pains - physical, mental or emotional suffering or torment, struggles

Beliefs - an opinion or conviction

Validation - substantiate; confirm

Business plan - a business plan is a written document that describes an idea for a product or service and how it will make money. It may include plans for marketing, expected profit, and expenses.

Pitch/Elevator Pitch - a brief talk or speech intended to sell or win approval for something

Introduction

I'm so excited that you have begun the path of building your legacy. I just want to share a little nugget of information that I learned along the way to become an entrepreneur. Being an entrepreneur isn't ALL about the money. It's about getting a clear vision of the life you want to have and making it a reality. When you become an entrepreneur, it shouldn't be like an extra job. It's actually a change in mindset and lifestyle. It's allowing yourself to think outside the box even if your idea seems crazy to other people. It might seem impossible at first until you find a way to make a profit from it. Your ideas are not crazy...they're courageous!

In order to take your generation into a mindset shift _From Brainstorm to Business_, you have to be equipped with an entrepreneurial set of skills and strategies that can be TAUGHT, LEARNED and MASTERED!

I hope you use the information in this book to guide you into a world of following your curiosity without limits!

Kathe Michele Hamilton

Brainstorming Questions

1. What are the things you like to do/hobbies?

```
[                                                              ]
```

2. What are the things people say you're good at/skills?

```
[                                                              ]
```

3. Which classes do you get your BEST grades are in?

```
[                                                              ]
```

Brainstorming Questions

4. Which classes do you enjoy learning in the most? Why?

5. What are the things that are needed in your community?

6. Who is an **entrepreneur** or **influencer** that inspires you? Why?

Brainstorm List

Now make a list of 5-10 possible businesses you could start, keeping in mind the skills, hobbies, and interests that you just answered in your **brainstorm** questions. This is how you find your **niche** (distinct area) in the business world. (For example, if your best grade is in Math, perhaps you start a Math tutoring business for students who are struggling in Math.)

1.
2.
3.
4.
5.
6.
7.
8.
9.
10.

Review your list. Which idea appeals to you the most? Why?

Journal Reflection

Now that you've had a chance to **strategically** brainstorm some ideas, let's process the information.

What have you learned about yourself?

┌───┐
│   │
│   │
│   │
│   │
│   │
└───┘

Did you notice whether your ideas involved providing a **product** or **service** or both?

┌───┐
│   │
│   │
│   │
│   │
│   │
└───┘

Was there a common theme that appeared from this brainstorming process? (For example, helping others, being creative)

┌───┐
│   │
│   │
│   │
│   │
│   │
└───┘

Validation

It's important to **validate** your ideas. Meaning, you need to know what your potential customers want. You want to create a business that meets the needs of what people want or need.

The best way to to find out what people want is to ask them!

Hop on the internet (you're probably already on it, lol). Choose your social media platform of choice. Start posting questions about the ideas you brainstormed in your brainstorming list. Here's how you might post a question:

"Hey friends/family I'm doing some research on businesses and I want to get your opinion. Would you use or but _____ Why? or Why not?"

Practice writing your own if you prefer:

What kind of response did you get from posting your questions on social media?

Research and Analyze

Social media is all good but you also need to research and analyze your business idea. Use Google and Amazon to search what businesses have already been created on the idea that you're most interested in. (For example, Math tutoring business)

Record your finding in the chart below:

Type of Business	Website	Pricing	Comments

Journal Reflection

What did you learn that surprised you the most? Why?

Were there several businesses or very few businesses in your research about your business idea?

Could you see yourself starting a business similar to the ones you researched? Why or Why not?

Target Audience/Market

No matter what business you start, you must know WHO your potential customers are. Look at it this way. It would be pointless to try and sell a car to a 5-year-old right? They can't drive it, they most likely don't have the money to buy it, and are probably not interested in purchasing a car yet.

You must know the who, what, when, where, and why about your potential customers. This information becomes the **audience** (people) you **target** for promoting your business and the **market** (the demand for your service or product) that you sell to.

Now, to get even more specific about your **target audience**, you can create a **consumer avatar**. This is a profile of your IDEAL customer who would love to buy your products or services.

Complete some basic information about your consumer avatar:

Are they male or female?

What is their age range?

Where do they like to go to eat, shop, hang-out?

What clothing **brands** do they like, wear or buy?

Are they **employed** or **unemployed**?

Where do they go for entertainment? (Movies, concerts, clubs, etc…)

What's their favorite social media platform?

Do they follow any influencers? If so, who are they?

Your Unique Offer

Once you have a grasp of WHAT and WHO you're selling to, now you need to understand how your consumer avatar feels. I know this might sound odd, but this is probably the most important part of being an entrepreneur. Your product or service must make a connection with a customer in order for them to even notice your business in a sea of competing similar businesses that are also available to them. In business, we say a potential customer needs to KNOW, LIKE, and TRUST you before they decide to do business with you.

You have to be in sync with the **pains** and **beliefs** of your consumer avatar. What you offer for sale must speak to their struggles or problem and they have to believe your business will solve that struggle or problem for them. (For example, let's say I failed my 9th Algebra class and I believe in order for me to get better in Math, I should get a Math tutor. I might hire you over other tutors because your unique offer states that you specialize in students that are failing and you have a tutoring system that will move my grade up in one semester or the next semester of tutoring is 50% off). Now it's your turn!

Create a unique offer for YOUR avatar's pains and beliefs. Here's a sentence frame and a sample to help you but you can also make up your own:

"_____ need _____
because they are struggling to find _____
They believe _____
I offer _____ to help _____
_____ so they can _____".

Sample:

" <u>Failing Algebra students</u> need <u>a culturally relevant tutor</u> because they are struggling to find <u>confidence in school</u>. They believe <u>they will never improve their grades and are giving up hope of every passing their class.</u> I offer <u>a culturally responsive tutoring system to help build their self-esteem</u> so that they can <u>become successful in improving their grades</u>"

Reflection Journal

What's going to make your business stand out from the rest?

What can they get from YOUR business that they can't get from other businesses?

Why should they trust your product or service?

How can you create KNOW, LIKE, and TRUST with a stranger so they will buy from your business?

Test Your Offer

Testing, testing, 1, 2, 3 testing! It's time to see if your offer is something that speaks to the target audience you have chosen.

Create a survey or poll with the group people that you are targeting to get their feedback on your offer. (For example, you might share your offer in an email or social media post asking people to rate it on a scale of 1-10 on whether they would be interested in your business based on that offer). *Google Forms* is a great tool for creating surveys.

Once you get the data from your survey/poll, tweak and revise your offer as needed according to the feedback you receive.

Create 1-5 questions about your offer for your survey/poll:

1.
2.
3.
4.
5.

Revise your offer if needed:

Reflection Journal

Did you target the right audience?

```



```

Did you provide enough information in your offer to sway them into being a customer?

```



```

Do you need to re-evaluate the product or service that you're selling?

```



```

What's Your Plan?

What is a business plan? A **business plan** is a written document that describes an idea for a product or service and how it will make money. It may include plans for marketing, expected profit, and expenses.

Think of a business plan like a map or brochure of an amusement park. You want to know what's in the park before you decide to go. You want to know the height requirements, places to eat and have an idea of how much everything is going to cost right? So it's the same with a business. You plan out the various aspects of your business so that there aren't any huge surprises! It helps to think about the costs that come with the business BEFORE diving in. It also lets people know you're serious about becoming an entrepreneur.

Here are just a few of the basic elements of a business plan to consider:

- ❏ Business Name
- ❏ Type of Business/Idea
- ❏ Demographics
- ❏ Marketing
- ❏ Promotions
- ❏ Advertisements
- ❏ Financing
- ❏ Start-up Costs
- ❏ Expenses
- ❏ Sale Price of product/service **(minus)** Cost to provide product/service **(equals)** Profit

Fill in your basic business plan to get you started below:

Business Name	
Type of Business/Idea	
Demographics	
Marketing	
Promotions	
Advertisements	
Financing	
Start-up Costs	
Expenses	
Profit	

Branding, Logo, and Marketing

Branding and creating your **logo** is an important part of marketing your business. It's like introducing yourself to someone for the first time. First impressions matter. This is how strangers get to KNOW you. Over time people will know your brand and become familiar with what products or services your business offers. With that being said, you want your brand and logo to represent who you are and the quality of service that your brand offers in the market. Do you want to market your business as a boring piece of boiled chicken with no flavor or a crispy juicy piece of chicken with some lemon pepper seasoning? Now, I'm hungry!

Consider words, phrases, and symbols for your branding, logo, and marketing. Complete your brand and logo brainstorming below:

What are 3 words that describe your business?

1.	
2.	
3.	

What phrases describe your business?

Sketch a design of your logo. You may use pictures, words, symbols or a combination of all.

Option #1

Option #2

Create a marketing plan of action for your business (daily, weekly, monthly):

Daily	Posts	Blogs	Videos	Emails	Other
SAMPLE	Instagram Twitter	Facebook	Snapchat Youtube	Friends Family	
Monday					
Tuesday					
Wednesday					
Thursday					
Friday					
Saturday					
Sunday					

Reflection Journal

How do you want to show up on the various social media platforms? Posts, Blogs, Videos, Print Ads?

```



```

How often and when is the best time to post about your business?

```



```

What kind of promotional materials do you need for your business? Business cards, posters, website?

```



```

Pitching Your Business

A **pitch or elevator pitch** is a brief (usually 20-60 seconds), a persuasive statement that you use to spark interest in what your business is and what you offer. People have a million things to do, and rarely have time to listen to a full speech about why they should buy something from your business. So creating a pitch is an easy way to Keep It Simple Students (KISS). If someone is interested, then they will ask you more about it or say no thank you and move on!

Create a pitch for your business idea:

Sample: *"I offer tutoring to students to help them improve their grades so that they can pass their A-G classes".*

Give it a try below. Remember to keep it brief. Time yourself. Only about 30 seconds is best!

Time Management
"If you FAIL to plan, you PLAN TO FAIL"

Learning how to effectively manage your time to create your business is a crucial skill so that you can offer the best products and services to your customers. Here are a few things to consider when managing your time:

1. Know your goals and stay true to them

What are your short- and long-term goals for your business? You should be scheduling a time to work on tasks and activities that directly relate to building your business...DAILY!

2. Prioritize your tasks (Make checklists)

Must Do-- Do them right away so you don't worry about it.

May Do-- It's your decision to do them or not but at some point, they should get done.

Choices--- trolling social media OR research your business by reading, webinars, podcasts, workshops, get coaching, writing content, journaling/planners and field study of your business.

3. "NO" is just a 2-letter word

If you have to say NO every once in a while, it's okay and your friends should be supportive of that in order for you to take care of what's truly important TO YOU...building your business!

```


```

4. Plan ahead

Night time activities-- Plan your outfit, pack your lunch, gather all the belonging you need for school at the front door AND pack your Business Journal/Planner. Decide what small task you will be working on during your break after-school or at home when you have free time. (Exploring the internet for competitor's strategies, listening to a podcast or webinar/FB live video, jotting down ideas to make your business unique).

```


```

5. Distractions take you off task

Start figuring out when your quiet time is. When all your homework or chores are taken care of and you can work on your business.

```


```

6. What are your TIME WASTERS?

Where or what are you spending most of your time on? (shopping, hanging out, texting, watching youtube) How can you maximize that time more efficiently? Delete 1 hr. from that time to devote to your business.

7. It's your time to SHINE!

Making better decisions on how to incorporate YOUR GOALS into your life every day will drive your motivation to bring your entrepreneurial dreams to life.

" What is achievable in your life is based on the beliefs you give yourself"

About the author

I have had the pleasure of being an educator for over 25 years at the elementary and secondary school level. I have a B.S. Degree in Child Development and a M.A. Degree in Educational Administration. During my educational career, I have had the opportunity to be a mentor teacher to several new teachers and I have supported teachers across the school district as an Instructional Coach.

In addition to being an educator, I stepped out on faith from 2008-2010 to start my first business. My sister and I both shared a love for cooking with our families and wanted to create a business that would combine our experience with teaching kids and making great food. Before we knew it, our ideas of opening a cooking school for kids turned into a real business plan and *The Kids Cooking Place* was born!

Creating my own business from the ground up was one of the best experiences of my life. Several years later, I decided to document the journey that we took to open our business so that it can serve as a guide to help other teachers become teacherpreneurs too! In 2016, I self-published my first book on Amazon, *Make Money Teaching Cooking Classes: A Guide to Start Your Own Kids Cooking Business*. Once I published my first book, I was hooked and went on to publish four more books and counting...

Ever since I was a little girl, whenever someone asked me what I wanted to do or be when I grew up, I always gave the same answer:

I want to be a teacher, have five kids, be a stay-at-home mom with a maid, own my own business and live on a farm!

Well, I can check-off half of those things so far... (only one child and too old for more, lol). I'm working on getting that farm before I retire though. I've said all of this to say, I became an entrepreneur because not only do I have an innate motivation to fulfill my dreams, but I also enjoy helping others work to their potential.

In fact, I started a side hustle coaching business, www.KatheMichele.com where I teach students and educators like myself how to build their own side hustle business while still working their teaching jobs. I provide new entrepreneurs with inspiration and information to pursue their entrepreneurial dreams.

Best wishes on your entrepreneurial journey!

Kathe Michele Hamilton

Made in the USA
Las Vegas, NV
30 July 2022